How Many Frogs?

Help!

Hope...

Lessons Learned...

How Many Frogs Do I Have to Kiss?

Help, Hope and Lessons Learned

Dawn D. Fobbs, CPC

Fobbs Group, LLC Self Discovery Books

How Many Frogs Do I Have To Kiss?
Help, Hope and Lessons Learned

Published by: Dawn D. Fobbs, CPC
              The Fobbs Group, LLC

              P.O. Box 6667
              Katy, Texas 77491

              (281) 858-9699 ofc
              (832) 201-7235 fax

              dawnfobbs.com

Copyright © 2008 by Dawn D. Fobbs

All rights reserved. No part of this book may be used or reproduced in any manner whatsoever without written permission of the publisher.

Edited by Robin Moore, Moore Communications

Cover Design by Kimberly Washington

Artwork by CMTmarketing.net

Distributed by:
    The Fobbs Group, LLC Self Discovery Books

Dedications

Dedicated To All Who Have Reach Out For Help, Experienced Hope and Learned A Few Lessons On The Path

This book is dedicated to all of the released frogs that have hopefully found true lasting love and meaningful relationships. And to the many frogs that have taught valuable lessons to many princesses!

This book is also dedicated to all of the great princesses in the meantime..................

Acknowledgements

To a wonderful team of professionals coast to coast. I appreciate Kimberly Washington with KT Marketing for her beautiful creativity in creating the book cover and back design, the incredible background work that takes to make a book on paper a reality in paperback.

To Robin Moore with Robin Moore Communications for meeting each deadline in the editing process such as phone calls, emails, and contract obligations. Your support was excellent!

Thank you to the more than 100 support resources it took to bring the point forth that we all learn something through the people we meet.

I acknowledge and thank the experts in the healthy relationship industry for their wisdom, guidance and resources (see page77-78)

And lastly, I acknowledge the men that have crossed my path and allowed me to teach them and for the wisdom they have passed on to me.

To each past relationship and welcoming all new relationships!!

Thanks to Pastor Creflo Dollar (as I was flipping the television stations), for reminding me in one of his sermons that sweet lips make a way for learning.

Say What?!?

Kiss a Frog?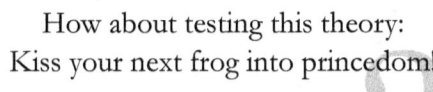

The Old Fairy tale that a frog prince is caught in an amphibian's body is just a wives' tale. If it were true, then you could kiss any frog and release a Prince, right?

> How about testing this theory:
> Kiss your next frog into princedom!

Ok, now that your lips are sore and your hope is down, REFRAME! Make a wish. Then take those lessons and remember what you are learning and have learned in the past.

Food for thought.........

"Most people who are looking for mates that they haven't quite found yet are so interested in getting to where they're going that they're missing the fun of going there."

> -- Abraham-Hicks
> Excerpt from a workshop in
> San Francisco, CA on Sunday, March 2nd 2007

"Lately my biggest problem has been that women are more concerned with the title of "girlfriend" or "wife" than they are with the man who makes it happen."

> - Essence Magazine, 2008
> Author Unknown

"No matter where you are relationally, I guarantee that you have learned something with each passerby."

- Dawn Fobbs

How many frogs have you kissed?

What have you learned and taught?

Where are you now?

What Inspired Me To Write This Book?

To encourage. Offer hope. Give a positive outlook on dating. Most importantly, to remind you to remember your lessons learned.

To discover the valuable lessons you may have taught.

To help you help yourself to not be Cinderella in reverse.

To inspire you to look for your desired mate in the meantime.

To help you reframe from spinning your wheels with frivolous dating, which encourages you to date people you can learn from.

"I can do better because I am better."

-Movie entitled "The Other Sister"

"I date not for the other person to make me happy.
I date people that add to my happiness
and fit into my lifestyle."

-Dawn Fobbs

FROM KISSING A FROG TO DISCOVERING YOUR PRINCE

Introduction   1

Chapter I   9
Introduce You To You, First

Chapter II   20
A Reason, A Season, A Lifetime
      Let The Kissing Begin

Chapter III   28
Getting Past Your Past
      Lessons Learned, Lessons Taught

Chapter IV   36
What Do You Really Want and
     How Bad Do You Want It?

Chapter V   47
Dating Tips and Considerations

Chapter VI   65
Keep learning. Keep Teaching. Keep On Kissing.

Chapter VII   71
What To Do With What You Have Learned

Chapter Summary   74

Affirmations, Related Resources, Humor   75-100

Introduction

Why would you kiss a frog?

It has been said that you've got to kiss a lot of frogs before you find your prince. Now you may be asking yourself "What frogs and where do they come from?" Let me help you to identify a prince when you get to know one.

As you read this book you will discover how important it is to keep moving forward while searching for your true prince. You will discover the importance of truly forgiving, why you should embrace each lesson or blessing, and most of all, how to know what to do when you make the decision to date once again in search of Prince Charming.

The story goes............
A handsome prince in a frog body desiring a beauty connects with, and comes to the rescue of, the damsel in distress. Once the damsel is discovered, it is his quest to liberate her from an evil spell.

Does this scenario bring back memories of other fairy-tales?

As the story continues..........
The frog kisses the damsel and becomes the handsome prince she is in need of and they live happily ever after. Have you ever kissed someone and knew he or she was the right one for you? Or, did you know immediately that he or she was not the one? If so, you are good, because it takes more than a kiss to tell if someone is the one with whom you should share your life. It takes time, a few other kisses, and a lot of experience with learning personalities.

If you are thinking you have wasted kisses or time, you are wrong. Just because this frog myth was read to you, it doesn't make it your reality. As for myths, here are a few international opinions about frogs to ponder as you read this book of hope and help.

Frog myths to ponder……………………..

In Australia, frogs are considered rain-makers. You know rain-maker humans make great things happen to change the direction of a current situation.

In India, frogs are meant to be cloud related. You know what a cloudy day feels like.

In Japan, frogs symbolize good luck. Think of the Lucky Charm symbol and the luck from wearing a Jade necklace.

Folklorists say, "If you see a green frog or toad the first day of Spring, you will have many tears shed throughout the year." Wow! Have you ever shed tears over a frog?

Some even associate frogs with evil. **No comment**!

What kinds of frogs have you kissed?

Or, are you the frog to become Prince Charming once experience is yours?

Great Affirmations Shared

"I do not have to earn love. I am lovable because I exist! Others reflect the love I have for myself."
-Louise L. Hay 1989

"I deserve the best and I accept the best NOW!"
-Unknown

Enjoy and Take Notes!

Write down your own feelings

or experiences learned

from kissing a few frogs.

Notes:

_____

_____

_____

_____

_____

_____

_____

_____

Loving others is easy when I love and accept myself

Introduce You to You, First!

CHAPTER 1

Help Yourself First

Deal with your problems before you make them other people problems. When you have made the decision to leap into a relationship it should be well thought through. Do you know you? Do you know your personality type? Do you know what you are willing to accept or not?

Have you gotten to know you? If not, take time to work on you, first.

We may all have baggage that could stand to be organized and downsized by taking true evaluations of our experiences that have ultimately shaped our dating attitudes. As you evaluate yourself, sit still and evaluate your self-talk. That is the talk you say in your head about everything that happens in life around you. The negative chatter box can be tamed.

Dealing with you first is a huge reward to others as they get to know the "you" you want to be.

When you've got a lot to offer, you don't have to settle.

Offering yourself to a relationship should not be hastily done. Evaluate what you are offering. The offering could be as simple but great as enthusiasm, popping optimism, wealth, great ability to motivate or a deep circle of influence.

Settling leads to regret, bitterness, and a bad trail of negative energy that you are in control of from the start. Why do you suppose you keep repeating the same relationships?

What are you offering?

_____   _____

_____   _____

Have you ever settled? Why? Yes or no

_____   _____

_____   _____

Are you settling right now? Why? Yes or no

_____   _____

_____   _____

Re-evaluate the offering! (list your qualities, etc.)

_____   _____

_____   _____

List Ways You Can Deal With Your Problems To Insure Relationship Success:

_____

_____

_____

_____

_____

_____

_____

_____

_____

_____

Example: Hire a life coach to help eliminate the negative mental clutter and quiet the negative chatter box.
(Let Coach Fobbs help you!) Dawnfobbs.com or fobbs.com

A few ideas:

I will not date for one full year in order to reflect and prepare.

I will hire a therapist.

I will retain a life/relationship coach.

I will journal my way through my issues.

I will incorporate mentors for every area of my life.

I will record and realize my dating patterns as I journal about the past to lead me to a promising future.

What do you have to gain, lose, or offer from dating?

Gain:

_____   _____

_____   _____

Lose:

_____   _____

_____   _____

Offer:

_____   _____

_____   _____

REFLECTIONS

Ms. Dawn's Lesson From Frog #1

Real Love Is Always Instilled Forever

You never forget your first love. You can fall in love over and over again. You can marry and have a clan of babies. You can ward off relationships to work on yourself. You still will never forget your first love!

Was it love or was it a fantasized ideal of what you thought love was supposed to be?

Whatever you think of your first love, just remember that that may have bearing on what you feel the standard should be.

Reflection Time

Who was your <u>first</u> love?

_____

What did you learn?

_____

_____

_____

What did you teach?

_____

_____

What do remember? (Good and bad)

_____

_____

What do you want to learn in the future?

_____

_____

_____

What do you want to teach in the future?

_____

_____

_____

In The End These Things Matter Most

How Well Did You Love?

How Fully Did You Live?

How Deeply Did You Learn To Let Go?

Loving Others is easy when I love and accept myself

A Reason, A Season, A Lifetime

CHAPTER II

Dawn D. Fobbs 21

Let The Kissing Begin

A Reason

As you grow in relationships you begin to have many Ahas! Moments of why you are learning the lessons you experience.

You need to know that each person you meet has a purpose for your life. Nothing **JUST** happens!

You may not be thinking reason as life plays out, however, be sure there is a reason for all of your actions.

A Season

What is your favorite season? What is your least favorite season? This may seem silly, however, know that if you know yourself, it would be a great idea to go through all four seasons with your potential Prince Charming before you decide to rescue or be rescued.

A Lifetime

Now that the reasons are discovered and the lessons have been secured, you can now see clearly a lifetime of bliss.

Just remember that people come into your life for three reasons. A Reason, A Season, or a Lifetime.

Think about it!

A Reason....
            A Season....
                        A Lifetime....

Who are the people in your life?

Reason?

Name:_____

Reason:

_____

Name:_____

Reason:

_____

Name:_____

Reason:

_____

Season? (did you go through the four seasons?)

Name:_____

   Season: _____

Name:_____

   Season: _____

Name:_____

   Season: _____

Lifetime? (who is sticking with you?)

Name:

_____

Name:

_____

Name:

_____

Name:

_____

Name:

_____

REFLECTIONS
Ms. Dawn's Lesson From Frog #2

Love Can Change Into A Friendship For Life

In an episode of "Sex in the City," Carrie once asked the question, "If you love someone and you break-up, where does the love go?"

I believe it turns into a great friendship or it turns you loose to give to someone else. I also believe love is transferable and can be re-considered.

Where has your past love gone?

Who have you once loved and are now great platonic friends with?

Where do you think love goes once it is no longer between two people in an exclusive relationship?

From the Author: I would love to hear from you about your individual experiences. Please email your comments to, wherethelovegoes@mail.com.

HOPE...

Getting Past Your Past

Just as a snake sheds it's skin, we must shed our past over and

CHAPTER III

Lessons Learned, Lessons Taught

If you are not learning, you are definitely not living. As Millie Jackson's song says "Think back to your very first time." I'm asking you to just think of all of your first time(s) learning each lesson.

I am sure when you were dating who seemed to be <u>*the one*</u> you may not have thought this must be a lesson. Think about it now.

As you ponder on the lessons learned, try to rescue the lessons you taught. Yes, you are a teacher as well.

Just think, there are people out there right now telling someone about you and what you taught them, good or bad.

As you kiss your frogs and hope for the Prince Charming effect, you should be thrilled to learn and ecstatic to be a teacher.

What do you share with others in candid conversations about what you were taught?

_____

What will you admit you learned from each relationship?

_____

What do you think you taught?

_____

I have learned many valuable lessons...

I learned

_____

    From: _____

I learned:

_____

    From:: _____

I learned:

_____

    From:: _____

I learned:

_____

    From:: _____

I taught many lessons...

I taught:

_____

    To: _____

I taught:

_____

    To: _____

I taught:

_____

    To: _____

I taught:

_____

    To: _____

REFLECTIONS
Ms. Dawn's Lesson From Frog #3

What To Do After The Divorce, Break-up, Being On Strike From Dating

After the divorce, I knew I wanted to be a wife again, someday.

Once the bitterness turns sweet again, and the eyes dry up, the feeling of wanting to forgive for your own personal sake will occur. I approve and guarantee all of the above.

Once you put yourself out there to start seeking Prince Charming, you quickly discover that breaking up does occur and it is ok. You bounce back sooner than anticipated and there are no hard feelings. I approve and guarantee those statements.

When it is time to abandon the dating strike, get out of the house and go where the frogs are leaping. It's like I tell my mom who expresses she would like to start dating again, "If you want to meet someone, get out and live life. No one is just going to knock on the front door. Even the UPS man can no longer bring the packages inside the door!

Relationships are full of rich lessons and makes you more aware with each one.

—Dawn Fobbs

What Do You Really Want? How Bad Do You Want It?

The heart is like a garden. It can grow compassion or fear, resentment or love. The question is what seed will you plant there?

CHAPTER IV

Dawn D. Fobbs

Reality Check Yourself

Do you go after what you say you want and deserve?

Do you stick to the promises you make to yourself?

Do you have a plan to get and keep your Prince Charming?

If you answered yes to at least two of the above questions, great! You are on the right track.

If you answered no, well it is ok. You can and will get there. Discovering "you" is a process that depends on your willingness. How to get there is your decision and the process has to be one that fits with your overall style. You have to decide to take action and work at it until you are totally comfortable with the daily process.

How badly do you want your Prince Charming?
Taking action will include making sure your baggage is minimal, clearing your mental path to have a great "you" to offer your prince, and putting in detail (on paper) what your idea of Prince Charming would look and feel like.

Be bold in reality checking yourself! Do it starting today. Put it on paper! Get who you say you want! As the slogan for J.P. Morgan Chase Bank says, "Chase what matters."

Keep in mind, you matter. What you want matters.

Help For Finding Your Prince Charming

Questions to ponder………….

What do you really want in your Prince Charming?

How badly do you want to meet the real Prince Charming?

What will you do to clear your mental path to attract the prince you are seeking?

What do you have to offer to the prince once he arrives?

Yes, he will arrive!

If you search certain keywords such as matchmaking, dating services, singles activities, etc., in 2008 there were 733,000 resources to help you find your Prince Charming.

For Example, here are a few.

www.match.com
www.eHarmony.com
www.singlesnet.com
www.datehookup.com

There are singles groups in every community.

Join a special interest club: Sierra Club, Fine Arts, Sports, etc.

In 2008 according to Google.com there were over 115,000,000 single's associations in US.

Put the word out:
Tell your friends and family you are interested in finding your Prince Charming. Ask them if they know anyone?

REFLECTIONS
Ms. Dawn's Lesson From Frog #4
No Turning Back

I am constantly amazed once a relationship has ended that the other party never gives up hope that there will be something possible in the future. The truth is, some people are so focused on what happened the first 3-6 months that they forget the whole story, especially the end result. You know, the reason the relationship ended.

I do believe in love at first sight. Do you?

As I recall, it happened to me in 1995 and, of all places, at the court house, in downtown Houston, Texas.

All I remember is I noticed someone that noticed me, a connection was made and four years later we were no longer a couple. Fast forward 14 years down the road he has never given up. He has never given up after he has a couple of ex-wives, a few children, a current wife and the knowledge that there will be no repeat of what we once had.

I knew that that relationship was for a reason and went for many seasons and proved to me that he was not the prince for me.

I am grateful for frog #4 because he is constantly teaching me that I do not want someone who has someone else. I do not want a man who will lie to his wife. I do not want a man who is emotionally unavailable and wants me because the though of someone else winning my heart is to much for him to handle.

Frog #4 never asked why I moved on many years ago. The reason is because he was emotionally unavailable and was not willing to commit to a monogamous relationship for life.

LESSONS

LEARNED...

Other Valuable Lessons From The Frogs Of Ms. Dawn's Relationships Past

- The curly haired frog taught me to never let anyone bring you down because I can do better. I taught him to enjoy happiness while it lasts.

- The Pepsi driver frog taught me to really trust my instincts and to give my all even if the other person does not deserve it. I taught him to realize that the grass is not greener on the other side.

- The barber frog taught me to never date anyone who is not past their past. I taught him that people do not have to play by negative rules.

- The muscle-bound frog taught me to never settle even when you know you could make it work. I taught him that non-stability will not keep the girl.

- The African frog taught me to appreciate what I do and to let people spoil you. I taught him to be with whom he really wanted not who was available at the time.

- The seventh grade frog in middle school taught me to take a chance and find what you do like. I taught him he was worthy to have a pretty girl. (me!)

- The chocolate covered frog taught me to keep my head on straight and let others be free to move on in their own way. I taught him that people get tired of being treated badly and they will happily move on toward
happiness.

- The last frog of all taught me to allow people to prepare the way for you to be better, wiser, and in a position to know what you want and deserve. I taught him to give his all while you have it to give and I also taught him what it was to really live in bliss.

These lessons are etched in my "do not repeat" log and are past appreciations. Every frog that has leaped my way has been greatly appreciated and I am grateful to share this with you for reading this book.

Love in the past is only a memory. Love in the future is a fantasy.
Only here and now can we truly love.

Dating Tips For Your Consideration
CHAPTER V

Be Prepared to Kiss and Be Kissed

"Prepared is the one who meets opportunity head on."

-Dawn Fobbs

Note To Men: Don't love the one you are with because you can't love the one you want.

_____

_____

_____

_____

Note To Women: A piece of a man is not better than no man at all. I Promise.

_____

_____

_____

_____

The Tips Before The Tips

Tips that you may not be ready for a long-term or meaningful relationship

- You are only bothered on event nights as a party date.
- The relationship you are currently in seems very platonic.
- You are a standing date at specific events and you give or get no other dates.

Finally:
- No rules are established, upfront or as the relationship progresses.
- No discussions regarding relationship growth or moving forward occurs.
- You keep looking for who is looking for you, while you are still connected to someone else.
- You avoid the big (where are we in this relationship) talk
- You keep dating the "<u>Allele 324</u>" male cheating gene guy. Yes, they have a name for it. Although it's not been proven, there may be some truth to this if you think about it. (Goggle.com!)

Like A Carrot Dangled Before A Horse, There Is Love, Just Out Of Reach!

-Dr. Robert Anthony
Author of: "Total Confidence"

Dating Power Tip

Re-group, disconnect, introduce "you" to you again. Start over and make yourself available for who is really available for you.

Remember: A _Reason_, A _Season_, A _Lifetime_. *(re-read Chapter 2)*

Quick reminders
- Dating is only a stepping stone, not the end of the road.
- Past -- Is gone and vague
- Future -- Not happening yet, prepare for the best!
- Don't fall in love for money, go where the money is to fall in love!

How about doing "Frunch?"
Frunch is not in the dictionary but is commonly defined as fast brunch or lunch. This method should be used when you are meeting someone for the first time and you do not want to be alone for too many hours or you just want to kill the blind date horror.

Questions??????

Do you typically throw out the "hang with me vibe" or do you make it clear that you are looking for a meaningful relationship?

How do you sabotage your dates? Oh, let's count the ways…………..

Do you accept pity dates?

Do you date only when you are bored?

Do you go on dates just to show off your new outfit?

Do you go on the date with low expectations?

Do you go only for the free meal and drinks?

Do you go on the date, get the meal and have your friend call with a fake emergency so you can leave?

More Tips To Help You Know When The Time Is Right

Check off each that applies to you. You decide if you're ready.

__ Groom well and look your best.

__ Know your position. Let the man be the man and you play your role.

__Allow your date to hold your hand when crossing the street.

__Recognize a good listener when it occurs.

__Be treated with respect in private and public.

__Friendliness is in the air!

__You can just be you without extra animation.

__Have a sense of humor and enjoy laughing.

__Be liable and trustworthy by your actions.

__Never kiss on the first few date. Kissing leads to other emotions.

__If you go online, take your time and make the first date a double date.

Cont....

__Be patient and do not plan the wedding before the third date.

__Honesty really is the best policy for a lasting relationship.

__If you participate in a blind date, send a picture of yourself by email before the date and request the same in return.

__Always make the first date a public adventure between 11:00 am and 2:00 pm.

__Never arrive late to a date. Never!

__Never discuss the ex's.

__Do not fake who you really are and scale back the flirting.

__Turn your cell phone on vibrate so you are fully present in a dating situation.

__Don't discuss marriage on the first date or reveal he is the one for you.

__Accept compliments by saying "thank you," and smile.

__Enthusiasm goes a long way.

__Try not to seem so nervous.

__State your intentions after you go through the four.

Notes:

_____

_____

_____

_____

_____

_____

_____

What The Top 7 Experts Say......

Dr Ruth Westheimer
"You can either give in to negative feelings or fight them, and I'm of the belief that you should fight them."
www.drruth.com

John Gray
"Just as women are afraid of receiving, men are afraid of giving."
http://home.marsvenus.com

John Welwood
"A conscious relationship in my view is one that puts you completely to the test as a human being." (KPFA Interview)
www.johnwelwood.com/index.htm

David Deida
"We eventually learn that emotional closure is our own action. We can be responsible for it. In any moment, we can choose to open or to close."
www.deida.info

John Gottman
"I liken an affair to the shattering of a Waterford crystal vase. You can glue it back together, but it will never be the same again."
www.gottman.com

Dr. Laura Schlessinger
"Don't spend time beating on a wall hoping to transform it into a door."
www.drlaura.com

Dr. Michelle
"One of the things you can do to kick off your plan to change your love life is a home makeover." (Article written for Book for Better Living)
www.drmichelle.com

Words from people I've met on marriage and dating:

"It is risky to fall in love."

"I am not getting any younger."

"At the end of the day, you need someone at home for you."

"I haven't made that choice, yet."

"I don't want to grow old alone."

"I just want to date with no attachments."

"I am looking for a few good men."

"I do want children…..eventually."

"I am afraid of marriage because it ties people together legally and emotionally."

"I do not want to be alone the rest of my life."

"I want the American dream, the kids, home, cars, etc."

"I like dating but do not want to get married."

"Unless I meet a millionaire, I am not dating."

More chatter...................

There are three *rings* of marriage. From the Movie: "A Guy Thing"
> The engagement ring
>> The marriage ring
>>> The suffering

Let's re-phrase and describe the rings as:
The engagement ring
> The marriage ring
>> The honoring

Some of the biggest lies and excuses I've heard from friends and associates:

"I attract all the wrong singles with no personality."

"I do not have time to date because of my work schedule."

"I cannot get involved until I finish school, the children leave home, or I make partner."

"Online dating is for losers."

"I will date after I lose 20 pounds."

"I will date only if the other person is really wealthy."

The "NEW YOU" Dating Tips

Now that you've gone through the self reflection from the previous pages…..

<u>Relax</u>: Don't be anxious and too hungry.

<u>Relate</u>: Learn communication skills

<u>Release</u>: Let go of all negative things of the past year.

*Even Loss And Betrayal Can Bring
Us Awakening.*
                          -Buddha

Keep Learning, Keep Teaching Keep on Kissing

CHAPTER VI

How Many Frogs Do I Have to Kiss? 66

Learn , Teach Kiss and Kiss

The learning begins from the moment you see someone. You are told to be attracted to the brain, intelligence and even kindness. However, reality is that the visual takes over each time. The immediate senses such as eyes, ears and emotions are heightened.

For instance, typically when you see that you are attracted, you are tempted to get closer to look for a ring and a   possible smell of cologne and the rhythm of the individual's voice. From those moves, you learn a few tidbits that linger in the brain even if you never get to actually meet the person formally.

Your actions, words, and body language will teach people what they need to know about you on the surface. So, be careful what you do, say, and show in public. Look back at all of the relationships you have been in and ask yourself "What did I teach?" As you talk about the other person, be aware that at some point they have discussed you. Observing behavior is sometimes better than language.

How many frogs will you kiss before you get your prince?

Just keep on kissing.
> Keep on teaching.
>> Keep on learning.

How To Know When It Is Time To Move On

In some relationships, we hold on because we are remembering all of the past good times and not being accountable for the misery that is currently taking place. I had a good friend Andy Valadez who once said, "People are loyal to things and they can't even explain why." Personally, when I made the decision to get a divorce, it was because I was given a great intuition that if I stayed, I would be older and bitter and not given an opportunity to get my joy back and live the life I really wanted to live in peace.

Look around you and listen to the language of married people that are not happy. Most will make remarks about sticking around for the children, referencing how many years have been spent together, how they got flowers in the beginning even though they have not received any attention in years, and most popular are the remarks about we have an "open" understanding.

No matter what, you deserve to be with people who want to be with only you and only share their attention relationally with you.

Here are a few hints you may need to move on

- It's been more than 3-5 years and no ring has appeared in any fashion.

- You both dance around any conversation about the next level of the relationship.

- The relationship is noticeably not moving forward.

- You have put your partner on a zero tolerance program, again.

- You can actually count how many times you are together, monthly.

- You have to keep reminding the other party that you are actually a couple.

- One of you is always avoiding the relationship conversation.

- Holidays bring stress because of false expectations.

- You are both over the age 40 and do not know how to introduce one another in public.

- You make the decision each year to discuss the issue and you back out each time.

- You do not take your partner to events because you want other potentials to notice you.

- You feel like you have to stay because you have put so much time into the relationship.

- You have actually started avoiding one another.

- You know you deserve better but you accept less because of physical attraction.

What to Do With What You've Learned

Get Your Mind Right! - *Dawn Fobbs*

The Mind Contains All Possibilities. - *Buddha*

CHAPTER VII

From Bitter to Better

Now that you have had some time to reflect, the time has come to consider what you will do with the ideas in this book or the ideas from your reflection and journaling time.

Whether you realize it or not, "You've come a long way baby!"

From bitter to better is where you want to be if you are truly serious about inviting a significant other into your world. The best gift to give to another is a joyful, happy, clear, positive, baggage-less, complete you.

It is very attractive to whoever is waiting to meet you when you have a great attitude and personality.

From bitter to better indicates that you were once one person and are now another. This transition also indicates you have done some amount of work on yourself to be a better you.

From bitter to better is also a great indication that you desire trying to be in a good place emotionally.

Congratulations for taking the time to work on you!

Chapter Summaries:

Chapter 1- Get to know you before you try getting to know someone else, relationally.

Chapter 2- Glance back at the lessons learned and categorize which ones were in your life for a reason, season, or a lifetime.

Chapter 3- Get past your past to insure a positive dating and possibly married future.

Chapter 4- How bad do you want what you say you want? Do your part and go for it!

Chapter 5- You make the rules. Get tips on how to be a great mate. Consider changing your current relationship pattern.

Chapter 6- Don't give up! Your time really is coming. Be patient and be fulfilled with your other passions. Keep busy in the meantime as to not settle.

Chapter 7- Learn, apply, and practice great habits.

Positive Affirmations To Remember

I welcome, and am open to receive all abundance that comes.

I am a confident and positive person, people gravitate
toward me everyday.

I am winning in all my relationships.

I am a positive and valuable contributor to my relationships.

What if the prince does not come?

Burned into my memory is a scene from the very popular show, Grey's Anatomy.

The episode is the one in which Meredith is hoping and wanting Derrick (Mr. McDreamy) will choose her over Allison. As the episode unfolds, there is a line that she so eloquently expresses, "Choose me! Pick me! Want me!"

I have to admit, I was in such a trance that I felt myself in that room with Meredith, and I just cried for her wanting and desperately pleading. For a moment, my heart forgot that this was just a show.

When I came back to reality as a commercial peeped in, I was crying for her more. I literally felt her emotion and that episode really wrapped me up for a few days. Here it is two years later, and I still remember that scene as if it played
today.

I took a vow to remember that episode as a reminder to never let that be me in that situation. I prayed and asked God to let someone want me as much as I want him.

Being divorced and single by choice is not easy. However, I will never settle to satisfy society or family members.

*There Is The Path of Fear and The Path of Love.
Which Will You Follow?*

*If You Let Cloudy Water Settle, It Will Become Clear.
If You Let Your Upset Mind Settle,
Your Course Will Also Clear.*

- Buddha

It didn't happen to you, it happened for you! There is always a lesson!

Share Your Story
Do you have a story to share about the lessons you have learned through dating, marriage or divorce?

We would love to hear about them to share with others to help them along the healing process.
Stories of.............
- Breaking up with your best friend you dated

- When you settled and knew you should not have

- Blind date horror stories

- Simple dating tips

- Single parents getting back into the dating scene

- What happened after you worked on you

- A time when you did not date for over a year

- If you love being single

- Your reasons for wanting to date or get married
- Now that you have found love
- Internet dating tips
- Who is your secret love interest?
- What valuable lessons will you pass on to loved ones?

Please share your first name only, age, and city.
Please email your submissions in 150 words or less to: howmanyfrogsdawn@mail.com

Release: By emailing your submission, you are agreeing to allow your story to be published on our website and possibly discussed in workshops, nationally. As all material sent will become the property of The Fobbs Group, LLC.

Notes:

_____

_____

_____

_____

_____

_____

_____

*If It Is Not An Adventure,
It Is Not Worth It!*

What The Kisses Mean In The End

To all of the men I have met that have taught me the most valuable lesson of all: I am better not bitter!

I am better because I have learned:
- How to say no and really mean it

- What I will and won't accept to be with another person

- How to be better for myself

- To expect and accept the best

- To continue to trust

- To treat each person individually and not compare

- To just be me

- When to say good-bye

- Boundary setting

- Not to look back

*To my daughters Aungelique and Paiton:
keep on believing in you and keeping
the faith in your dreams.*

Keep the...........

Faith

Patience

Life Learning

Experience

And look at positive examples around you.

And finally............

- No repeating after the break-up

Other Seminars and Self-Improvement Classes By Dawn Fobbs

Ms. Fobbs is available to speak to your group.

Dawn Fobbs is a multi-talented multi-faceted woman with a bright past and beaming future. As a speaker, authoress, life and business coach, business consultant and over-all entrepreneur for more than a decade, you are sure to learn from her wisdom. Dawn Fobbs has traveled nationally speaking, and coaching.

Dawn Fobbs performs an annual conference titled "Bring It Forth" Vision Planning 101 in Texas and would be delighted to inspire you to bring your talents and desires forth in your life.

To learn more about Dawn, visit dawnfobbs.com, dfobbs.com, or dawnfobbstv.com.

Fobbs loves traveling, writing, reading, and meeting new people. Dawn lives in Katy, Texas with her four children, Aungelique, Joshua, Sai'Vonne, and Paiton.

Email Ms. Fobbs at: dfobbs@dawnfobbs.com

29 Related Resources: Great CD's and Books To Read
(Please Read Them All and Then Some!)

CD- *The Law of Attraction*	*Abraham-Hicks*
Woman- An Intimate Geography	*Natalie Angier*
The Art Of Living	*Erich Fromm*
The Heaven-Sent Husband	*Devion Huey*
For Better Or For Better	*Gary Smalley*
The Relationship Dictionary	*Mattias Goransson*
The Four Agreements	*Don Miguel Ruiz*
Don't Sweat The Small Stuff In Love	*Richard Carlson, Ph.D.*
	Kristine Carlson
I Gave Dating A Chance	*Jeramy Clark*
The Power Of Unconditional Love	*Ken Keyes, Jr.*
Letting Go Of The Person You Used To Be	*Lamas Surya Das*
Born For Love	*Leo Buscaglia*
101 Ways To Get and Keep His Attention	*Michelle McKinney Hammond*
For Women Only	*Shaunti Feldhahn*
200 Ways To Balance Your Life	*Bret Nicholaus and Paul Laurie*

Change Magazine (Oct. 2009)
To The Single Ladies and Choosing A Mate
(taffiedollar.org)
(creflodollar.com)

Note: Read the "Change Magazine" Article on "Choosing A Mate" to review the 20 questions to ask before choosing a marriage partner.

Resources Continued..............

Getting Off The Emotional Roller Coaster
                    Bob Phillips
Freeway of Love   Jan Latiolais-Hargrave
Falling In Love For All The Right Reasons
                    Dr. Neil Carl Warren
DSI: Date Scene Investigation   Ian Kerner, Ph.D.
The Secret Ingredient   Jan Heller
The Man Plan   Whitney Casey
Realistically Ever After   Cristina Ferrare
What Men Really Want   Susan Crane Bakos
The Art of Kissing   William Cane
50 Ways To Meet You Lover/ Laurie Rozakis
50 Ways To Drop Your Lover
Find A Husband After 35   Rachel Greenwald
Happiness   Will Ferguson

How To Tell He's Not The One In Ten Days

                    Michele Alexander
                    Jeannie Long
Become A Better You   Joel Osteen

It is okay to make a list of your ideal mate and keep it near. Check your list often and keep on believing!

Despite the freeing of many frogs, I still truly believe there is a Prince Charming out there for me. The thing is, he doesn't know I exist, yet!

Summary: Where Am I Now?

The list does still exist. Although I am paying attention to my surroundings I am content with being single.

My faith is stronger than ever.

My patience has increased as I re-evaluate my happiness being single, by choice.

I am enjoying being me and helping others to discover themselves.

I am continuing to introduce me to me every day I breathe!

A Bit of Humor…..

Recognize A Good Woman

A good woman is proud. She respects herself and others. She is aware of who she is. She neither seeks definition from the person she is with, nor does she expect them to read her mind. She is quite capable of articulating her needs.

A good woman is hopeful. She is strong enough to make all of her dreams come true. She knows love, therefore she gives love. She recognizes that her love has great value and must be reciprocated. If her love is taken for granted, it soon disappears.

A good woman has a dash of inspiration and a dabble of endurance. She knows that she will, at times, have to inspire others to reach the potential God gave them. A good woman knows her past, understands her present and faces toward the future.

A good woman knows God. She knows that with God the world is her playground, but without God she will just be played with.

A good woman does not live in fear of the future because of her past.

Instead, she understands that her life experiences are merely lessons meant to bring her closer to self-knowledge and unconditional self-love

Source Unknown

Final Share: The List

A Little Something To Chuckle About

What I Want In A Man, **Original List**...... (at age **22**)
- Handsome
- Charming
- Financially Successful

- A Caring Listener
- Witty
- In Good Shape
- Dresses with Style

- Appreciates the Finer Things
- Full of Thoughtful Surprises
- An Imaginative, Romantic Lover

What I Want In A Man, **Revised List**...... (at age **32**)
- Nice Looking- preferably with hair on his head
- Opens car doors, hold chairs
- Has enough money for a nice dinner at a restaurant
- Listens more than he talks
- Laughs at my jokes at appropriate times
- Can carry in all the groceries with ease

- Owns at least one tie
- Appreciates a good home cooked meal
- Remembers Birthdays and Anniversaries
- Seeks romance at least once a week

What I Want In A Man, **Revised List**...... (at age **42**)
- Not too ugly- bald head ok
- Doesn't drive off until I am in the care
- Works steady- splurges on dinner at McDonalds on occasion

- Nods head at appropriate times when I'm talking
- Usually remembers the punch lines of jokes
- Is in good enough shape to re-arrange the furniture
- Usually wears shirts that cover the stomach
- Knows not to buy champagne with screw-top lids
- Remembers to put the toilet seat lid down
- Shaves on most weekends

What I Want In A Man, **Revised List**...... (at age **52**)
- Keeps his nose and ears trimmed to appropriate

length
- Doesn't belch of scratch in public
- Doesn't borrow money too often
- Doesn't nod off to sleep while I'm emoting
- Doesn't re-tell same joke too many times
- Is in good enough shape to get off couch on weekends
- Usually wears matching socks and fresh underwear
- Appreciates a good TV dinner
- Remembers your name on occasion
- Shaves on some weekends

What I Want In A Man, **Revised List**…… (at age **62**)

- Doesn't scare small children
- Remembers where the bathroom is
- Doesn't require much money for upkeep
- Only snores lightly when awake (Loudly when asleep)
- Forgets why he's laughing
- Is in good enough shape to stand up by himself
- Usually wears some clothes
- Likes soft foods
- Remembers where he left his teeth
- Remembers when

What I Want In a Man, **Revised List**...... (at age **72**)
- <u>**Breathing**</u>

(source unknown - another great email)

Question:
Santa Claus, the perfect woman, the perfect man and the Tooth Fairy get in to a car accident- - who survives?

Answer:
The perfect woman, because the other three don't exist!

Source Unknown

More fun and funny jokes....

The Guys' Rules

At last a guy has taken the time to write this all down. Finally, the guys' side of the story. (I must admit, it's pretty good.) We always hear "the rules" From the female side.
Now here are the rules from the male side. These are our rules!

Men are NOT mind readers.

Learn to work the toilet seat. You're a big girl. If it's up, put it down. We need it up, you need it down. You don't hear us complaining about you leaving it down.

Sunday sports. It's like the full moon or the changing of the tides. Let it be.

Shopping is NOT a sport. And no, we are never going to think of it that way.

Crying is blackmail.

Ask for what you want. Let us be clear on this one: Subtle hints do not work! Strong hints do not work!

Obvious hints do not work! Just say it!

Yes and No are perfectly acceptable answers to almost every question.

Come to us with a problem **only** if you want help solving it. That's what we do.

Sympathy is what your girlfriends are for.

A headache that lasts for 17 months is a problem.   See a doctor.

Anything we said 6 months ago is inadmissible in an argument. In fact, all comments become null and void after 7 Days.

If you won't dress like the Victoria's Secret girls, don't Expect us to act like soap opera guys.

If you think you're fat, you probably are. Don't ask us.

If something we said can be interpreted two ways and one of them makes you sad or angry, then we meant the <u>other one</u>

You can either ask us to do something or tell us how you want it done. Not both. If you already know best how to do it, just do it yourself.

Whenever possible, Please say whatever you have to say during commercials.

Christopher Columbus did NOT need directions and neither do we.

ALL men see in only 16 colors, like Windows default settings. Peach, for example, is a fruit, not A color. Pumpkin is also a fruit. We have no idea what mauve is.

If it itches, it will be scratched. We do that.

If we ask what is wrong and you say "nothing," We will act like nothing's wrong. We know you are lying, but it is just not worth the hassle, besides we know you will bring it up again later.

If you ask a question you don't want an answer to, Expect an answer you don't want to hear.

When we have to go somewhere, absolutely anything you wear is fine...Really.

Reader Notes:

Notes:

Reader Notes:

Notes:

_____

_____

_____

_____

_____

_____

_____

From The Authoress

Think about what a blessing you have been in the lives of others. You deserve to have what you desire in a mate. If you are content being single, that is ok as well. Work on you so you will be ready when time permits.

In the meantime, love the life you have been afforded!

Dawn D. Fobbs

Authoress Bio

Dawn Fobbs is an energetic entrepreneur who loves to share experiences with those that are confused about life and the lessons you are learning each day.

As a professional coach, her specialty in confidence building and results based action methods.

With over a dozen business ventures. She has been a an entrepreneur since 1999 and has taught professionals the essence of being, doing and having what they say they want.

Fobbs is a professional consultant, national
speaker and enthusiastic self-published authoress of more than a dozen books and growing.

THE END

To order additional Books Contact:

The Fobbs Group, LLC
P.O. Box 6667
Katy, Texas 77491
(281)-858-9699

A complete list of books may be found at:
www.dfobbs.com
www.dawnfobbs.com